KU-737-577

First published in Great Britain 2022 by Farshore
An imprint of HarperCollins*Publishers*
1 London Bridge Street, London SE1 9GF
www.farshore.co.uk

HarperCollins*Publishers*
Macken House, 39/40 Mayor Street Upper,
Dublin 1, D01 C9W8, Ireland

©2022 Pokémon. ©1995–2022 Nintendo / Creatures Inc. / GAME FREAK inc.
TM, ®, and character names are trademarks of Nintendo.
All rights reserved.

ISBN 978 0 0085 0954 5
Printed and Bound in the UK using 100% renewable electricity at CPI Group (UK) Ltd
004

Written by Emily Stead.

A CIP catalogue record for this book is available from the British Library.

All rights reserved. No part of this publication may be reproduced, stored in a retrieval system,
or transmitted in any form or by any means, electronic, mechanical, photocopying, recording
or otherwise, without the prior permission of the publisher and copyright owner.

Stay safe online. Farshore is not responsible for content hosted by third parties.

This book is produced from independently certified FSC™ paper
to ensure responsible forest management.

For more information visit: www.harpercollins.co.uk/green

CODE BREAKERS

Join Ash, Goh and Pikachu as they travel far and wide in search of new and exciting Pokémon!

You'll meet hundreds of special species as you journey across the eight known Pokémon regions – from Alola to Unova, Kanto to Galar.

Try your hand at the head-scratching codes and challenging ciphers to become an expert Pokémon Trainer. The Poké Balls at the top of each page tell you how difficult a puzzle is. Turn the page to begin your journey.

Get cracking, Trainer!

POWERFUL PSYDUCK

Crack the code to learn which three Pokémon Psyduck will face in battle. Which one do you think Psyduck's Psychic-type moves will be most powerful against?

A	B	C	D	E	F	G	H	I
	Y					T		

J	K	L	M	N	O	P	Q	R
				M				

S	T	U	V	W	X	Y	Z
						B	

1. _ _ _ _ _ _
U V V Y Z H

2. _ _ _ _ _ _ _
S Z D O F X S Z

3. _ _ _ _ _ _
O Z K I Z H

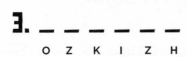

Psyduck is strongest against: ....

Because: ....

RISE AND SHINE!

Use the zigzag cipher to work out how to wake this sleepy Pikachu. Start at the left, then copy the letters into the box below.

R N I S M B R I S

B I G T O E E R E

_ _ _ _ _ _ _ _ _ _ _ _ _ _ _ _ _ _
_ _ _ _ _ _ _ _ !

7

GOH WILD!

Goh's Pokémon sure has grown since they began their journey to Galar's Wild Area. Circle every second letter to reveal the name of the Pokémon whose pebble-juggling skills are legendary!

Start:

Answer: _ _ _ _ _ _ _ _ _, _ _ _

_ _ _ _ _ _ _ _ _ _ _ _

WANTED!

Team Rocket's ultimate mission is to steal Ash's Pikachu – this time they almost did it! Which trickster was caught red-handed? Crack the code, then unscramble the letters to put the culprit behind bars!

Jessie

A	B	C	D	E	F	G	H	I
	2		4			7		
J	K	L	M	N	O	P	Q	R
10			14					18
S	T	U	V	W	X	Y	Z	
					24	25		

James

13   23   5

8   20   15

_ _ _ _ _ _

Meowth

Help! Some letters have been replaced with symbols in the names of these Pokémon. Work out which symbol represents which letter to figure out the critters' names.

1. B  TT  RFR

2. P  NCH  M

3. S  ZZL  P  D

4. W ✴ ✴ L ✴ ✴

5. H  WL  CH

🥊	=	☐
🐗	=	☐
🔥	=	☐
✴	=	☐
💧	=	☐

JUNGLE JAUNT

Ash and Pikachu are exploring the lush jungles of the Alola region. Use the coordinates below to find letters in the grid, and reveal the Pokémon type they are most likely to encounter.

	a	b	c	d
4	G	S	L	R
3	M	I	Y	D
2	F	P	W	H
1	E	V	A	T

___ ___ ___ ___ ___
a4 d4 c1 b4 b4

___ ___ ___ ___
d1 c3 b2 a1

11

HIT THE WALL

Watch out – the rocket cannons that belong to Blastoise can blast through brick walls! Complete the addition wall, then discover a Pokémon that can defeat Blastoise using the code below.

Tip: Start from the bottom bricks and things will soon add up! For example, 7 + 13 = 20.

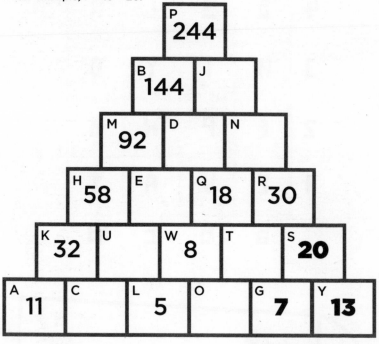

100, 3, 5, 10, 34, 3, 48

_ _ _ _ _ _ _

POKÉ BALL PROBLEMS

Meddling Meowth has scrambled the names of these nine powerful Poké Balls to avoid capture! Can you write the real names below?

TEARG

_ _ _ _ _

VIED

_ _ _ _

STEN

_ _ _ _

SKUD

_ _ _ _

HALE

_ _ _ _

CUKQI

_ _ _ _ _

TRALU

_ _ _ _ _

STEMAR

_ _ _ _ _ _

TNE

_ _ _

CODE GREEN

DIFFICULTY:

Ready, set, go! Complete the names of these Grass-type Pokémon to reveal the hidden name of a ninth!

1. I ☐ Y S A U R

2. F L A P P L ☐

3. L E A F E O ☐

4. B ☐ L B A S A U R

5. G O S ☐ I F L E U R

6. T H W ☐ C K E Y

7. L ☐ D I C O L O

8. G ☐ O O K E Y

☐ ☐ ☐ ☐ ☐ ☐ ☐ ☐
- - - - - - - -

14

LOOKING BACK

Sometimes information about new Pokémon appears in the most mysterious of places! Work out the back-to-front words written on the mirror, then write out the message below.

REPORTS SUGGEST THAT SNEASEL, THE CUNNING POKÉMON, EVOLVES INTO WEAVILE, THE SHARP CLAW POKÉMON.

. . . .

. . . .

. . . .

. . . .

. . . .

. . . .

MYSTERIOUS MASH-UPS

DIFFICULTY:

Rotom's data has become scrambled, mixing up Pokémon! Look at the screens and decide which creatures have been accidentally combined.

1.

ARCANOISE =

. . . .

&

. . . .

2.

BULBACHOMP =

. . . .

&

. . . .

MAKE A FACE

Take a look at these Pokémon patterns — which face should appear in the empty box in each row? Draw in the missing creatures.

1.

2.

3.

4.

This next cipher uses dots and dashes to send messages in secret! Can you decipher who's who using the Morse code below?

A .‒	G ‒‒.	M ‒‒	S ...	Y ‒.‒‒
B ‒...	H	N ‒.	T ‒	Z ‒‒..
C ‒.‒.	I ..	O ‒‒‒	U ..‒	
D ‒..	J .‒‒‒	P .‒‒.	V ...‒	
E .	K ‒.‒	Q ‒‒.‒	W .‒‒	
F ..‒.	L .‒..	R .‒.	X ‒..‒	

1. ‒‒. ‒‒‒ .... ☐

2. ‒.‒. .... .‒.. ‒‒‒ . ☐

3. .‒ ... . ☐

4. ‒.‒. .‒. ‒ ‒..‒ . ... ‒‒‒ .‒.
/ ‒.‒. . .‒. .. .. ☐

A. **B.** **C.** **D.**

DESTINATION: UNKNOWN

DIFFICULTY:

Add the missing letter in each Pokémon name to learn Ash and Pikachu's onward destination once they land in the Galar region.

1. R A L ☐ S
2. M A C ☐ A M P
3. S T ☐ E L I X
4. M E O ☐ S T I C
5. P ☐ K A C H U
6. J O ☐ T I K
7. P S Y ☐ U C K
8. L A P R ☐ S
9. S N O ☐ L A X
10. L E A F ☐ O N
11. P O N Y T ☐

TYPE TRANSLATOR

You may have met these Pokémon in the wild, but do you know their types? Try using this pigpen cipher to help you. To use the code, find the letter you need in one of the grids. Each part of the grid forms a shape for each letter. The first one has been done for you.

1.

P S Y C H I C

Dusclops

2.

Espurr

20

3.

Eevee

4.

Grubbin

5.

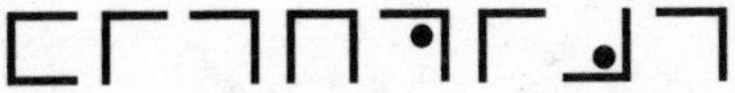

Pancham

6.

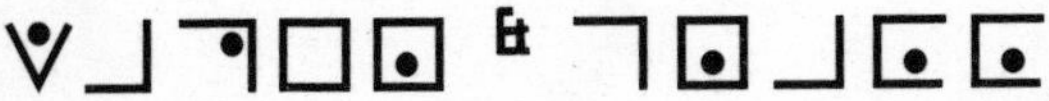

&

Ludicolo

7.

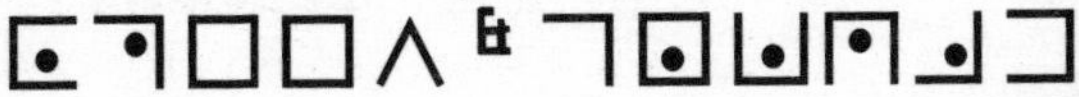

&

Steelix

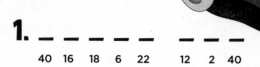

SNOOZE, YOU LOSE!

Complete the code below, then use it to work out the three moves that this snoozing Snorlax will use in its next battle!

A	B	C	D	E	F	G	H	I	J
	4	6							

K	L	M	N	O	P	Q	R	S	T
			30						

U	V	W	X	Y	Z
		48		52	

1. _ _ _ _ _   _ _ _
40 16 18 6 22   12 2 40

2. _ _ _ _ _ _ _ _
18 26 26 42 28 18 40 50

3. _ _ _ _ _ _ _ _
14 24 42 40 40 30 28 50

DEAR DIARY

DIFFICULTY:

To keep things private, Goh has written a coded entry in his diary.
Can you crack the code and write out the entry again?

> PKMY PKNEXT PKGOAL
> PKIS PKTO PKCATCH
> PKMEW, PKWHILE PKMY
> PKDREAM PKWOULD
> PKBE PKTO PKCATCH
> PKEVERY PKSINGLE
> PKPOKÉMON!

· ·

· ·

· ·

· ·

· ·

· ·

A LEGENDARY UPDATE

Rotom has the info on most Pokémon, but the entries for this Legendary pair have not yet been updated! Decode the numbers below to add the Pokémon names to Rotom's Pokédex. To find the right letters, first read along the grid, then go down.

1.

55 11 33 11 55 51 43 54 11

2.

55 11 31 42 11 43

	1	2	3	4	5
1	A	B	C	D	E
2	F	G	H	I	J
3	K	L	M	N	O
4	P	Q	R	S	T
5	U	V	W	X/Y	Z

A STUNNING SIGHT

DIFFICULTY:

Which Pokémon has Ash met in the wild today? Cross out any Pokémon with double letters in their names — the first one is done for you. The Pokémon that remains is the answer!

1.

GOSSIFLEUR

2.

. . . .

3.

. . . .

4.

. . . .

5.

. . . .

6.

. . . .

7.

. . . .

8.

. . . .

9.

. . . .

Ash has received a very mysterious message. When he first read it, it made no sense at all! Can you help? Pick out the letters in bold to reveal which Pokémon has been spotted flying over Vermilion Port.

LIKE **U**NOVA, **G**ALAR **I**S **A** TERRIFIC HABITAT – EXPECT LOTS OF EXTRAORDINARY SIGHTS! EACH NEW DAY, A ROVING YAMPAR PLAYS OR KIRLIA'S EPIC MOVES ASTOUND!

· ·

· ·

· ·

· ·

NUMBER CRUNCHING

Professor Cerise has set a new entry code at the lab, to keep out unwanted visitors! Gain entry by writing the numbers contained in the names of these Pokémon. The first number is written for you.

Tentacruel   Arcanine   Cottonee

Magnezone   Tentacool   Ninetales

Mewtwo   Litten   Cubone

The code is:

10 _ _ _ _ _ _ _ _

BACK-WORDS

Sometimes on a journey, you have to go backwards to move forwards! Crack the code that's being used below, then draw lines to connect the names with the correct Pokémon picture.

1. AKAMURAD

_ _ _ _ _ _ _ _

2. RATIVRAL

_ _ _ _ _ _ _

3. POHCAM

_ _ _ _ _ _

4. XINO

_ _ _ _

5. DRAZIRAHC

_ _ _ _ _ _ _ _ _

What do you notice about the names of these Pokémon?

6. EEVEE   **8. ALOMOMOLA**

7. HO-OH   **9. GIRAFARIG**

∙∙

∙∙

ON THE RIGHT TRACK

DIFFICULTY:

In the wild, tracking is a useful way of leaving signs or picture trails for other Trainers to follow. But first you need to decipher the code. Draw lines to connect these five tracking signs with their meanings.

A.

B.

C.

1. TURN RIGHT

2. DANGER

3. NO ENTRY

4. TURN LEFT

5. GONE HOME

D.

E.

MASTER OF DISGUISE

To become a top Trainer you'll need to put in a shift! The Caesar shift is a substitution cipher where the vowels are changed to the next one along.

VOWELS:		CODE:
A	=	E
E	=	I
I	=	O
O	=	U
U	=	A

IIVII
E E V E E

TYPE: ✓ NORMAL ☐ DARK

Use the cipher to work out Eevee's eight evolutions. Extra credit if you can name the Pokémon types!

1. FLERIUN

_ _ _ _ _ _ _

TYPE: ☐ FIRE ☐ WATER

2. JULTIUN

_ _ _ _ _ _ _

TYPE: ☐ GROUND ☐ ELECTRIC

3. LIEFIUN

_ _ _ _ _ _ _

TYPE: ☐ POISON ☐ GRASS

4. GLECIUN

_ _ _ _ _ _ _

TYPE: ☐ ICE ☐ FIRE

5. ISPIUN

_ _ _ _ _ _

TYPE: ☐ DARK ☐ PSYCHIC

6. SYLVIUN

_ _ _ _ _ _ _

TYPE: ☐ FAIRY ☐ STEEL

7. AMBRIUN

_ _ _ _ _ _ _

TYPE: ☐ FIGHTING ☐ DARK

8. VEPURIUN

_ _ _ _ _ _ _ _

TYPE: ☐ WATER ☐ DRAGON

31

POISON PRINT

Ivysaur are colourful creatures, but also pretty poisonous! Add some colour to this photo of an Ivysaur using the colour code to help you.

1 = pink	**4** = green
2 = light blue	**5** = brown
3 = blue	**6** = black

TAKE FLIGHT

A Butterfree flight is a lovely sight! Solve the number sentences, then cross out the correct answers in the grid. Put the remaining numbers in order from smallest to largest to show how many Butterfree there are.

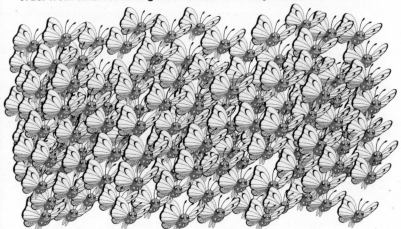

A. 9 + 8 = ☐

B. 70 − 50 = ☐

C. 4 x 4 = ☐

D. 12 ÷ 4 = ☐

E. 11 x 9 = ☐

F. 32 − 8 = ☐

16	4	3
1	20	5
24	17	99

Answer:

WATER WORK OUT

Get set to get wet when investigating Water-type Pokémon!
Work out the totals for the three Pokémon in each column
and row using the key below to help you.

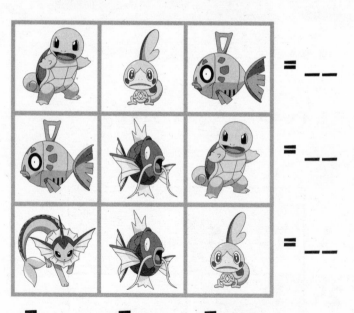

ARMOURED ATTACKER

Have you encountered this dangerous Pokémon? Its jaw can chomp through steel. See if you can solve the anagram in your head before tracing the paths.

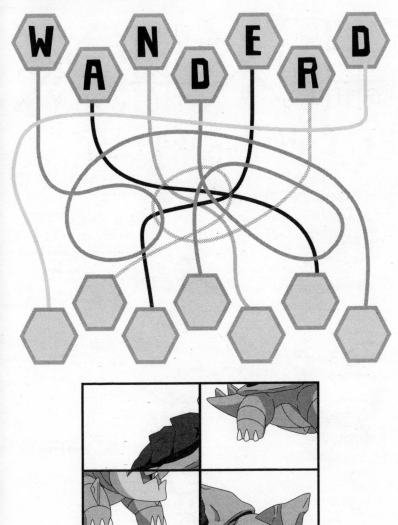

MAKE A CHANGE

DIFFICULTY: ⬤ ⬤

Pokémon are curious creatures that like to keep you guessing!
Use the pigpen cipher to work out which evolved form the
Pokémon below will take.

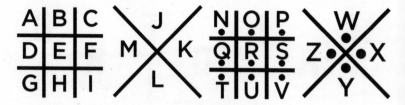

1.

Applin

⌐⌐∟∧□⌐⌐⌐⌐

_ _ _ _ _ _ _ _

2.

Eevee

⌐>⊔▫□⊔⌐

_ _ _ _ _ _ _ _

Something's not quite right with the names of these creatures! Use the pictures to help you figure out the Pokémon pairs that have been mixed up.

1.

CHARJAPUFF =

. . . .

&

. . . .

2.

RUFFDUCK =

. . . .

&

. . . .

CROSS WORDS

DIFFICULTY:

Take care when taking on a tearful Sobble – its moves can leave you weeping! Follow the instructions below to discover which of these four fearsome Pokémon can beat Sobble in battle.

Cross out any words that:
- are 6 letters long
- are only 2 letters
- are more than 8 letters long
- end in the letter S
- begin with the letter M

ALWAYS	USE	ESPURR	RALTS
BOLTUND	FEEBAS	BECAUSE	IF
TO	UNLESS	OF	FLYING
NORMAL	WATER	TYPE	CREATURES
POKÉMON	CRITTERS	ARE	MAINLY
LEGENDARY	MYTHICAL	WEAK	MASSIVE
HELPLESS	AGAINST	ELECTRIC	POISON
DRAGON	TYPE	POKÉMON	TRAINERS

CODED CLOCKS

Use the curious clock to find the names of three regions that Ash has visited. Write the letters that the minute hand is pointing to, followed by those that the hour hand is indicating. The last letter already appears!

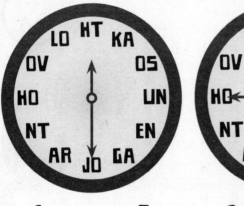

1. _ _ _ _ _ O

2. _ _ _ _ _ N

3. _ _ _ _ _ S

GHOSTED!

Six Ghost-type Pokémon have gathered, but a seventh has done a disappearing act! Find the sneaky spooks hiding in the grid.

P	G	S	C	I	M	Z	Q	N	C
D	L	E	V	K	D	X	J	H	M
X	U	H	N	B	N	P	L	A	I
A	F	S	Z	G	X	B	S	U	M
L	X	Q	K	W	A	P	V	N	I
L	K	O	D	N	O	R	Z	T	K
U	R	P	X	L	O	V	B	E	Y
K	E	D	C	M	B	I	N	R	U
S	C	S	H	J	K	W	R	W	Y
U	U	F	X	V	X	L	Q	Z	J
D	W	H	A	U	N	T	H	G	D

**DUSCLOPS   GENGAR
DUSKULL   HAUNTER
DUSKNOIR   MIMIKYU**

Rearrange the shaded letters to reveal
the Pokémon's name, then write it below.

— — — — —

TRACKING SKILLS

Rearrange the letters to find out which four Pokémon have made tracks. Then write the numbers in the boxes that match the creatures.

1.

- - - - - - -

2.

- - - - - - -

3.

- - - - - - -

4.

- - - - - - -

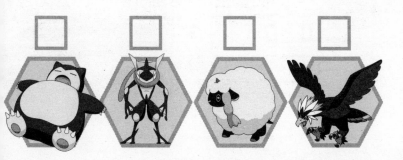

Charjabug the Battery Pokémon is powering up these computer monitors! Can you fill in the blanks on each screen to complete the binary code puzzles? The first puzzle has been completed for you.

RULES:

1. Each box should contain either a zero or a one.

2. More than two equal numbers immediately next to or below each other are not allowed.

3. Each row and each column should contain an equal number of zeros and ones.

4. Each row is unique and each column is unique – any row cannot be exactly equal to another row, and any column cannot be exactly equal to another column.

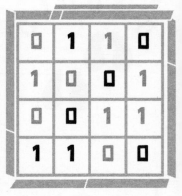

A.

B.

1		1		0	0
	0				
				0	
0		0		1	1
0					1
	1		0		

C.

		0		0		0	1
	1	1		0			
						0	
0			1	1			
			1				0
1						1	
	0				0		
		1			0		0

S.O.S.

Ash is locked in the Cerise Laboratory with a shadowy Pokémon on the prowl! He quickly writes a message on the steamed-up window. Help Chloe read the backwards message and come to Ash's rescue.

MISSING LINK

While checking his supplies, Ash has discovered some of his stuff is missing! Study these Pokémon patterns, then draw the berry or Poké Ball that should appear in each row.

1.

2.

3.

4.

45

GO WITH THE FLOW!

Hanging out by a volcano makes these six sizzling Pokémon feel fired up! But when the lava flows, it's time to go! Write down the coordinates when you spot each Fire-type Pokémon in the grid. To you get started, Vulpix is in square G4.

Vulpix

Charmander

Charmeleon

Charizard

Flareon

Scorbunny

TREASURED BERRIES

DIFFICULTY:

How do you make friends with a Pokémon? Remember to always carry some berries! Complete the code, then use it to help you work out the names of the four delicious berries below.

A	B	C	D	E	F	G	H	I	J	K	L	M
2	4		8		12				20			

N	O	P	Q	R	S	T	U	V	W	X	Y	Z
	30	32			38						50	

1.

30 36 2 28

= _ _ _ _

2.

40 2 26 2 40 30

= _ _ _ _ _ _

3.

32 10 6 16 2

= _ _ _ _ _

4.

38 18 40 36 42 38

= _ _ _ _ _ _

47

Study the close-ups of the first three Pokémon, then write down their names. Use the first letter of each name to discover what the New Species Pokémon is called.

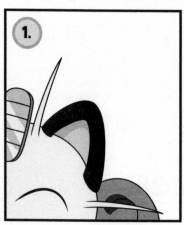

1.

2.

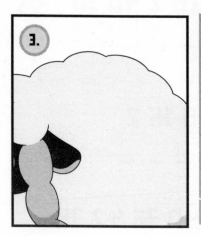

3.

4.

NEW SPECIES
POKÉMON:

TYPE TABLES

Study the key below, then use it to help you puzzle out the ten multiplication questions. Good luck, Trainer!

FIRE	ELECTRIC	GRASS	WATER	DRAGON	FIGHTING
= 1	= 2	= 3	= 4	= 5	= 6

STEEL	BUG	ROCK	ICE	NORMAL	PSYCHIC
= 7	= 8	= 9	= 10	= 11	= 12

A. ⚡ ☐ x 🐉 ☐ = ☐

B. ❄ ☐ x 🌿 ☐ = ☐

C. 🔮 ☐ x 💧 ☐ = ☐

D. 🐉 ☐ x 🪨 ☐ = ☐

E. 🐛 ☐ x ⚡ ☐ = ☐

F. 🌿 ☐ x ❄ ☐ = ☐

G. 🥊 ☐ x ✴ ☐ = ☐

H. ⚙ ☐ x ⚡ ☐ = ☐

I. 🔥 ☐ x 🐛 ☐ = ☐

J. 💧 ☐ x 💧 ☐ = ☐

49

A hidden message surrounds this Great Ball with some good advice for any Trainer! Circle every second letter to reveal what it reads.

Start:

Answer: _ _ _ _ _ _ _ _ _ _ _ _ _

_ _ _ _ _ _ _ _ _ _ _ _ _ _ _ _!

SPLASH LANDING

Complete the names of seven Water-type creatures to reveal the name of an eighth – the most beautiful Pokémon of them all!

1. ☐ AGIKARP

2. SQU ☐ RTLE

3. WARTORT ☐ E

4. VAP ☐ REON

5. BLAS ☐ OISE

6. GREN ☐ NJA

7. LUDI ☐ OLO

☐

_ _ _ _ _ _ _

Ash's mum Delia has sent her son an email, but Pikachu keeps hopping on to the keyboard while Ash is trying to read it! Delete the letters P and C to read Delia's message.

PTPRACICN
HPAPRCD,
PANDC PLOOCK
PACFTERP
YOPURC
YELPCLOWP
BCUDPDY!

DEINO'S DOTS

DIFFICULTY:

Another Morse code puzzle for you to decipher, Trainer! Decode the phrase below to discover Deino's secret.

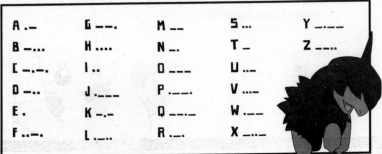

A .—   G ——.   M ——   S ...   Y —.——
B —...   H ....   N —.   T —   Z ——..
C —.—.   I ..   O ———   U ..—
D —..   J .———   P .——.   V ...—
E .   K —.—   Q ——.—   W .——
F ..—.   L .—..   R .—.   X —..—

....

....

....

....

....

The types of these ten Pokémon have been changed using the Caesar shift – where the vowels are changed to the next one along. Use the cipher to work out the Pokémon types.

VOWELS:	CODE:
A = E	
E = I	
I = O	
O = U	
U = A	

1.

FORI

_ _ _ _

2.

OCI

_ _ _

3.

ILICTROC

_ _ _ _ _ _ _ _

4.

WETIR

_ _ _ _ _

5.

NURMEL

_ _ _ _ _ _

6.

DERK & OCI

_ _ _ _ & _ _ _

7.

FOGHTONG & STIIL

_ _ _ _ _ _ _ _ & _ _ _ _ _

8.

DERK & DREGUN

_ _ _ _ & _ _ _ _ _ _

9.

RUCK & GRUAND

_ _ _ _ & _ _ _ _ _ _

10.

PSYCHOC & FEORY

_ _ _ _ _ _ _ & _ _ _ _ _

TOTALLY TRICKY

From which Onix did the steely-eyed Steelix below evolve? Add up the numbers on each Onix, then find the one that matches Steelix's total.

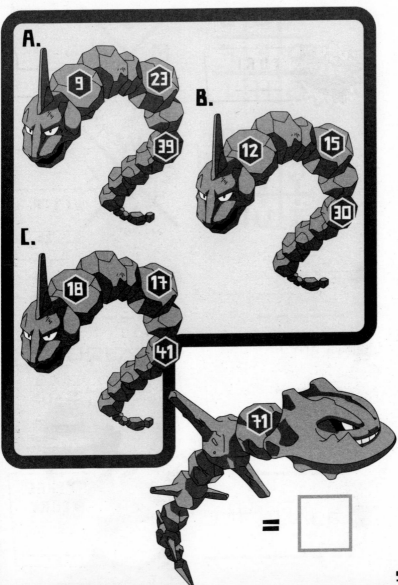

A. 9 23 39

B. 12 15 30

C. 18 17 41

71 =

Besides Team Rocket, Ash has faced some tough teams in the different Pokémon regions. Work out the team names using the pigpen cipher.

A	B	C
D	E	F
G	H	I

J · M · K · L (in X grid)

N•	O•	P•
Q•	R•	S•
T•	U•	V•

W• · Z• · X• · Y• (in X grid with dots)

1.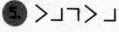

_ _ _ _ _

2.

_ _ _ _ _ _

3.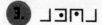

_ _ _ _

4.

_ _ _ _ _

5.

_ _ _ _ _

6.

_ _ _ _ _ _ _ _

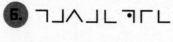

CRIED AND SEEK

DIFFICULTY:

Ash, Goh, Pikachu and Raboot are hiding to avoid the tears of a weeping Sobble . . . when it cries, everyone cries! Write down the coordinates when you spot each character in the grid.

Ash

Goh

Pikachu

Raboot

CRYPTIC CREATURES

Complete the names of these six puzzling Pokémon by drawing a line to the missing part of its name.

___CHOMP

LAX

___KULL

DUS

SNOR___

GAR

___DEVOIR

___CLOPS

MUNCH___

Do you have expert evolution knowledge?
Tick true or false below.

	TRUE	FALSE
1. Snorlax evolves into **Munchlax**.		
2. Duskull evolves into **Dusclops**.		
3. Garchomp evolves into **Gardevoir**.		

CLAWED CRITTER

This cruel critter fights tooth and claw! Try to solve the anagram in your head before tracing the paths.

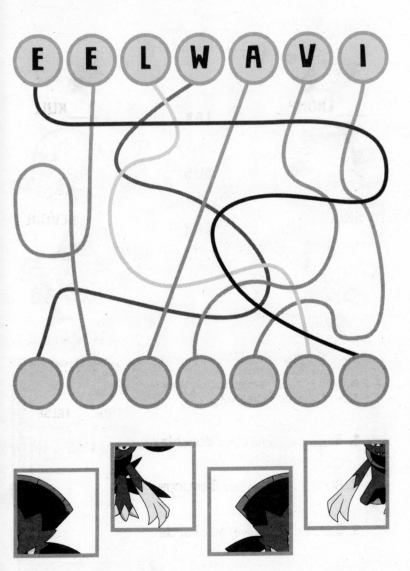

E E L W A V I

CHILLY CHALLENGE

DIFFICULTY:

Circle every second letter to learn another name by which Glaceon, an incredible Ice-type Pokémon, is known.

Start:

TIMELY TEST

Write the letters that the minute hand is pointing to, then the ones shown by the hour hand. They combine to complete the names of three more fascinating Pokémon regions. The last letter is written for you.

1. _ _ _ _ _ O

2. _ _ _ _ A

3. _ _ _ _ R

If you want to solve this next puzzle, Trainer, you might want to take a step backwards instead of forwards. Complete the alphabet key, then try to work out the names of the five aquatic Pokémon pictured.

A	B	C	D	E	F	G	H	I	J	K	L	M
Z					G							

N	O	P	Q	R	S	T	U	V	W	X	Y	Z
	N	O								W		

1. NBHJLBSQ = _ _ _ _ _ _ _ _

2.  TUVOGJTL = _ _ _ _ _ _ _ _

3.  NJMPUJD = _ _ _ _ _ _ _

4. TPCCMF = _ _ _ _ _ _

5. XBSUPSUMF = _ _ _ _ _ _ _ _ _

ASH'S AIM

DIFFICULTY:

Ash is a Trainer on a mission – but what exactly is it? Use the zigzag cipher to discover his ultimate dream!

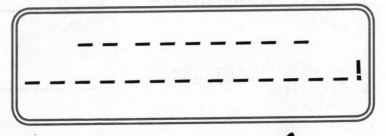

O E O E P K M N A T R

T B C M A O É O M S E

_ _ _ _ _ _ _ _ _

_ _ _ _ _ _ _ _ _ _ _ _ _ !

BACK TO WHERE IT ALL BEGAN!

DIFFICULTY: 🔴

What amazing adventures Ash and Pikachu have had, travelling the world in search of Pokémon! Safely home in Pallet Town, let's look BACK and name the eight regions they have visited.

1. OTNAK

_ _ _ _ _

2. OTHOJ

_ _ _ _ _

3. NNEOH

_ _ _ _ _

4. HONNIS

_ _ _ _ _ _

5. AVONU

_ _ _ _ _

6. SOLAK

_ _ _ _ _

7. ALOLA

_ _ _ _ _

8. RALAG

_ _ _ _ _

BY THE BOOK

The book cipher is a code that isn't easily cracked! Here, you'll use the pages of this book to work out a hidden message. Are you ready to take on your final challenge?

Example:

To find the word that is encoded

64-1-2

- turn to **page 64**
- look at the **first line**
- count along until you find the **second word**, which is "amazing"!

50-1-10   10-2-4   53-1-9

42-2-3   65-2-1

64-1-10   23-2-5 **!**

.... , ...

....

.... **!**

SOLUTIONS

POWERFUL PSYDUCK

PAGE 6

A	B	C	D	E	F	G	H	I	J	K	L	M
Z	Y	X	W	V	U	T	S	R	Q	P	O	N
N	O	P	Q	R	S	T	U	V	W	X	Y	Z
M	L	K	J	I	H	G	F	E	D	C	B	A

1. Feebas
2. Hawlucha
3. Lapras

Water-type Psyduck is strong against
Fighting and Flying-type, Hawlucha.

RISE AND SHINE!

PAGE 7

BRING IT SOME BERRIES!

GOH WILD!

PAGE 8

The Pokémon is:
CINDERACE, THE STRIKER POKÉMON.

WANTED!

PAGE 9

The culprit is: MEOWTH.

A	B	C	D	E	F	G	H	I
1	2	3	4	5	6	7	8	9
J	K	L	M	N	O	P	Q	R
10	11	12	13	14	15	16	17	18
S	T	U	V	W	X	Y	Z	
19	20	21	22	23	24	25	26	

LOST LETTERS

PAGE 10

1. BUTTERFREE
2. PANCHAM
3. SIZZLIPEDE
4. WOOLOO
5. HAWLUCHA

= A

= E

= I

= O

= U

JUNGLE JAUNT

PAGE 11

The Pokémon type that Ash and Pikachu are
most likely to encounter is: GRASS TYPE.

HIT THE WALL

PAGE 12

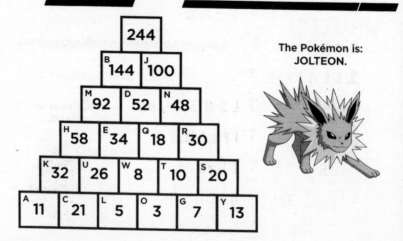

The Pokémon is:
JOLTEON.

244

B 144 J 100

M 92 D 52 N 48

H 58 E 34 Q 18 R 30

K 32 U 26 W 8 T 10 S 20

A 11 C 21 L 5 O 3 G 7 Y 13

POKÉ BALL PROBLEMS

PAGE 13

GREAT

DIVE

NEST

DUSK

HEAL

QUICK

ULTRA

MASTER

NET

CODE GREEN

PAGE 14

1. I **V** Y S A U R

2. F L A P P L **E**

3. L E A F E O **N**

4. B **U** L B A S A U R

5. G O S **S** I F L E U R

6. T H W **A** C K E Y

7. L **U** D I C O L O

8. G **R** O O K E Y

The Pokémon is:
VENUSAUR.

69

LOOKING BACK

PAGE 15

> REPORTS SUGGEST THAT SNEASEL, THE CUNNING POKÉMON, EVOLVES INTO WEAVILE, THE SHARP CLAW POKÉMON.

MYSTERIOUS MASH-UPS

PAGE 16

1. Arcanine & Blastoise

2. Bulbasaur & Garchomp

MAKE A FACE

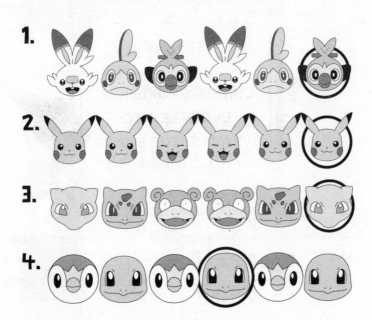

1.

2.

3.

4.

GET THE MESSAGE

1. D – Goh

2. C – Chloe

3. B – Ash

4. A – Professor Cerise

1. RAL **T** S
2. MAC **H** AMP
3. ST **E** ELIX
4. MEO **W** STIC
5. P **I** KACHU
6. JO **L** TIK
7. PSY **D** UCK
8. LAPR **A** S
9. SNO **R** LAX
10. LEAF **E** ON
11. PONYT **A**

They will travel to: THE WILD AREA.

1. PSYCHIC
2. GHOST
3. NORMAL
4. BUG
5. FIGHTING
6. WATER & GRASS
7. STEEL & GROUND

SNOOZE, YOU LOSE!

A	B	C	D	E	F	G	H	I
2	4	6	8	10	12	14	16	18

J	K	L	M	N	O	P	Q	R
20	22	24	26	28	30	32	34	36

S	T	U	V	W	X	Y	Z
38	40	42	44	46	48	50	52

1. THICK FAT
2. IMMUNITY
3. GLUTTONY

DEAR DIARY

MY NEXT GOAL IS TO CATCH MEW, WHILE MY DREAM WOULD BE TO CATCH EVERY SINGLE POKÉMON!

1.

ZAMAZENTA

2.

ZACIAN

1. GOSSIFLEUR
2. SCORBUNNY
3. EEVEE
4. FLAPPLE
5. WOOLOO
6. STUNFISK
7. GRUBBIN
8. BUTTERFREE
9. ESPURR

The Pokémon is: STUNFISK (GALAR FORM).

LUGIA THE
LEGENDARY
POKEMON

NUMBER CRUNCHING

The code is:
10, 9, 1, 1, 10, 9, 2, 10, 1

Tentacruel Arcanine Cott**onee**

Magnez**one** **Ten**tacool **Nine**tales

Mew**two** Litten Cub**one**

BACK-WORDS

1. DARUMAKA
2. LARVITAR
3. MACHOP
4. ONIX
5. CHARIZARD

6-9: The Pokémon names read the same forwards as they do backwards.

ON THE RIGHT TRACK

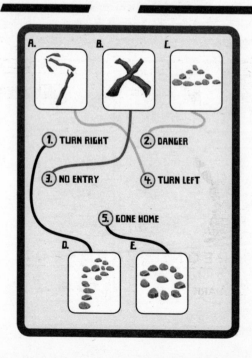

A. B. C.

1. TURN RIGHT
2. DANGER
3. NO ENTRY
4. TURN LEFT
5. GONE HOME

D. E.

MASTER OF DISGUISE

PAGES 30-31

1.

F L A R E O N

☑ FIRE

2.

J O L T E O N

☑ ELECTRIC

3.

L E A F E O N

☑ GRASS

4.

G L A C E O N

☑ ICE

5.

E S P E O N

☑ PSYCHIC

6.

S Y L V E O N

☑ FAIRY

7.

U M B R E O N

☑ DARK

8.

V A P O R E O N

☑ WATER

TAKE FLIGHT

A. 9 + 8 = 17   **D.** 12 ÷ 4 = 3

B. 70 - 50 = 20   **E.** 11 x 9 = 99

C. 4 x 4 = 16   **F.** 32 - 8 = 24

There are

1	4	5

Butterfree.

WATER WORK OUT

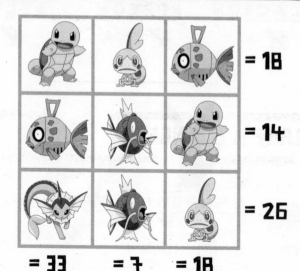

= 18

= 14

= 26

= 33   = 7   = 18

78

ARMOURED ATTACKER

PAGE 35

MAKE A CHANGE

PAGE 36

 1. Applin **A P P L E T U N**

 2. Eevee **U M B R E O N**

1. Charjabug & Jigglypuff

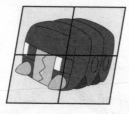

2. Rufflet & Psyduck

CROSS WORDS

~~ALWAYS~~	USE	~~SEADRA~~	~~RALTS~~
BOLTUND	~~FEEBAS~~	BECAUSE	~~IF~~
~~TO~~	~~UNLESS~~	~~OF~~	~~FIXING~~
~~NORMAL~~	WATER	TYPE	~~CREATURES~~
POKÉMON	~~CRITTERS~~	ARE	~~MAINLY~~
~~LEGENDARY~~	~~MYTHICAL~~	WEAK	~~MASSIVE~~
~~HELPLESS~~	AGAINST	ELECTRIC	~~POISON~~
~~DRAGON~~	TYPE	POKÉMON	~~TRAINERS~~

CODED CLOCKS

PAGE 39

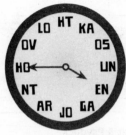

1. JOHTO **2. HOENN** **3. KALOS**

GHOSTED!

PAGE 40

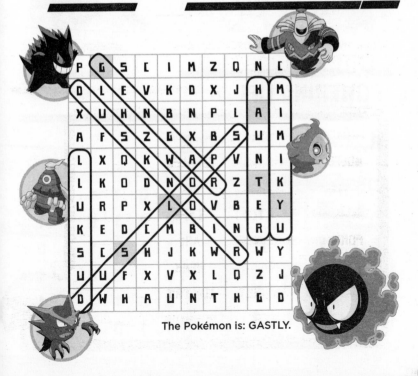

The Pokémon is: GASTLY.

TRACKING SKILLS

PAGE 41

1. <u>WOOLOO</u>   2. <u>GRENINJA</u>

3. <u>BRAVIARY</u>   4. <u>SNORLAX</u>

POWERING UP!

PAGES 42-43

A.

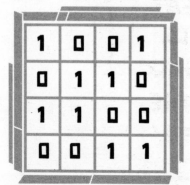

1	0	0	1
0	1	1	0
1	1	0	0
0	0	1	1

B.

1	0	1	1	0	0
0	0	1	0	1	1
1	1	0	1	0	0
0	1	0	0	1	1
0	0	1	1	0	1
1	1	0	0	1	0

C.

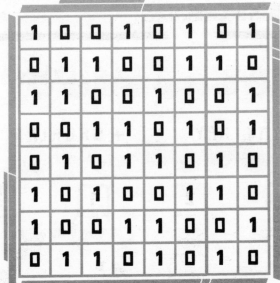

S.O.S.

PAGE 44

GRAB A GREAT BALL, GENGAR ON THE LOOSE!

MISSING LINK

PAGE 45

1.

2.

3.

4.

GO WITH THE FLOW!

PAGE 46

The coordinates are:

Vulpix	G4
Charmander	E2
Charmeleon	D4
Charizard	B6
Flareon	A1
Scorbunny	C3

TREASURED BERRIES

PAGE 47

A	B	C	D	E	F	G	H	I	J	K	L	M
2	4	6	8	10	12	14	16	18	20	22	24	26
N	O	P	Q	R	S	T	U	V	W	X	Y	Z
28	30	32	34	36	38	40	42	44	46	48	50	52

1. = ORAN

2. = TAMATO

3. = PECHA

4. = SITRUS

NEW SPECIES

PAGE 48

1. MEOWTH

2. EEVEE

3. WOOLOO

4. NEW SPECIES POKÉMON: MEW

A. ⚡ 2 × 🌸 5 = 10

B. 🏵 10 × 🌿 3 = 30

C. 🔮 12 × 💧 4 = 48

D. 🌸 5 × 💎 9 = 45

E. 🍬 8 × ⚡ 2 = 16

F. 🏵 10 × 🏵 10 = 100

G. 🥊 6 × ✴ 11 = 66

H. ✈ 7 × ⚡ 2 = 14

I. 🔥 1 × 🍬 8 = 8

J. 💧 4 × 💧 4 = 16

Answer: <u>U S E</u> <u>A</u> <u>G R E A T</u> <u>B A L L</u>
<u>F O R</u> <u>Y O U R</u> <u>N E X T</u> <u>C A T C H</u>!

1. **M** AGIKARP
2. SQU **I** RTLE
3. WARTORT **L** E
4. VAP **O** REON
5. BLAS **T** OISE
6. GREN **I** NJA
7. LUDI **C** OLO

The Pokémon is:
MILOTIC.

MUM'S THE WORD

PAGE 52

TRAIN
HARD,
AND LOOK
AFTER
YOUR
YELLOW
BUDDY!

The message reads:
TRAIN HARD AND
LOOK AFTER YOUR
YELLOW BUDDY!

DEINO'S DOTS

PAGE 53

Deino's secret: IT GAINS AN EXTRA HEAD
EACH TIME IT EVOLVES.

TAKE TEN

PAGE 54

1.

FORI
FIRE

2.

OCI
ICE

3.

IL ICTROC
ELECTRIC

4.

WETIR
WATER

5.

NURMEL
NORMAL

6.

DERK
& OCI
DARK
& ICE

7.

FOGHTONG
& STIIL
FIGHTING
& STEEL

8.

DERK
& DREGUN
DARK
& DRAGON

9.

RUCK
& GRUAND
ROCK
& GROUND

10.

PSYCHOC
& FEORY
PSYCHIC
& FAIRY

TOTALLY TRICKY

PAGE 55

= A

TESTING TEAMS

1. SKULL
2. PLASMA
3. AQUA
4. FLARE
5. MAGMA
6. GALACTIC

CRIED AND SEEK

PAGE 57

The coordinates are:

Ash

Goh

Pikachu

Raboot

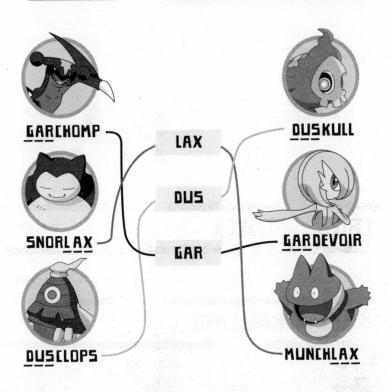

GARCHOMP

LAX

DUSKULL

SNORLAX

DUS

GARDEVOIR

GAR

DUSCLOPS

MUNCHLAX

	TRUE	FALSE
1. Snorlax evolves into **Munchlax**.		✔
2. Duskull evolves into **Dusclops**.	✔	
3. Garchomp evolves into **Gardevoir**.		✔

CLAWED CRITTER

PAGE 59

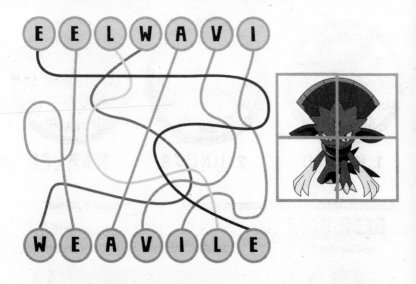

E E L W A V I

W E A V I L E

CHILLY CHALLENGE

PAGE 60

THE FRESH SNOW
POKÉMON.

TIMELY TEST

PAGE 61

1. K A N T O

2. U N O V A

3. G A L A R

DEEP DIVE

PAGE 62

A	B	C	D	E	F	G	H	I	J	K	L	M
Z	A	B	C	D	E	F	G	H	I	J	K	L

N	O	P	Q	R	S	T	U	V	W	X	Y	Z
M	N	O	P	Q	R	S	T	U	V	W	X	Y

1. MAGIKARP
2. STUNFISK
3. MILOTIC
4. SOBBLE
5. WARTORTLE

> ## TO BECOME A POKÉMON MASTER!

1 KANTO

2 JOHTO

3 HOENN

4 SINNOH

5 UNOVA

6 KALOS

7 ALOLA

8 GALAR

50-1-10   10-2-4   53-1-9

42-2-3   65-2-1

64-1-10   23-2-5 !

GOOD   WORK, TRAINER.

YOU   CRACKED

THE   CODE   !